CRAFT ★ STAR

PET Crafts

Everything You Need to Become Your Pet's Craft Star!

By Megan Friday

Walter Foster Publishing, Inc.
3 Wrigley, Suite A
Irvine, CA 92618
www.walterfoster.com

This library edition published in 2012 by Walter Foster Publishing, Inc.
Distributed by Black Rabbit Books.
P.O. Box 3263 Mankato, Minnesota 56002

Printed in Mankato, Minnesota, USA by CG Book Printers, a division of Corporate Graphics.

First Library Edition

Library of Congress Cataloging-in-Publication Data

Friday, Megan.
  Pet crafts : everything you need to become your pet's craft star! / by Megan Friday. -- 1st
library ed.
     p. cm. -- (Craft star ; cst11)
  ISBN 978-1-936309-41-2 (hardcover)
  1. Handicraft--Juvenile literature. 2. Pet supplies--Juvenile literature. I. Title. II. Title: Everything you need to become your pet's craft star!
  SF413.5.F75 2011
  745.592--dc22
                                                                           2011008874

042011
17320

9 8 7 6 5 4 3 2 1

PET
Crafts

By Megan Friday

Table of Contents

Meet Megan

A self-taught crafter, Megan Friday enjoys doing anything creative—including knitting, sewing, paper crafts, cooking, and photography. Megan was an early childhood educator for 12 years before taking time to raise her son and daughter. She currently juggles freelance crafting with her many responsibilities as a doting mom and devoted pet owner. When she has a free moment to spare, Megan enjoys hiking, traveling, reading, and studying child development. Her creative inspiration comes from her family and friends, animals, nature, and beautiful fabrics and prints. (She simply can't resist anything with stripes!) Megan is delightfully married to a graphic designer, and their family resides in Boulder, Colorado.

Let's Get Crafty!

Is your pet spoiled rotten? My Weimaraner Katie sleeps in my bed, suffers from separation anxiety, and watches way too much TV! It all began when I decided to add variety to her wardrobe with different hand-sewn collars. I noticed that Katie took on different personas in her collars: she became animated in her party collar and behaved regally when donning her purple crown collar. Nowadays, Katie gets to pick out her own collars and I have invented tons of other crafts that cater to her every whim.

If you are besotted with your pets and love finding new ways to show your adoration, then look no further, dear reader! This book guides you step by step through fun projects that allow you to creatively feed, clothe, pamper, and entertain your pets. Read on to discover how to become your pet's craft star!

Stuff You'll Need

Here are some of the supplies you'll need to complete the projects in this book. Keep in mind that each craft has its own materials list that you should check before beginning that project, as you want to be sure you have the correct sizes and quantities, and some items may not be covered in this section. To get started, gather the following basic tools: scissors, a pencil, a ruler, and a permanent marker.

Glues

Many projects involve sticking various things together, so make sure you have strong glues that work with paper, fabric, wood, plastic, and aluminum. I suggest getting craft glue, tacky glue, stretchy fabric glue, and different types of decoupage.

Fabrics

Some of the projects use felt, fleece, furry fabric, or tulle. However, feel free to experiment with other fabrics that let you share your favorite textures with your pet. I recommend keeping a needle, thread, and safety pins on hand as well.

Paper

In the following projects, you'll have the opportunity to work with a range of papers, such as gift wrap, tissue paper, colorful cardstock, and preprinted decorative paper. Photographs featuring your fabulous pets and favorite animals are also used in the crafts.

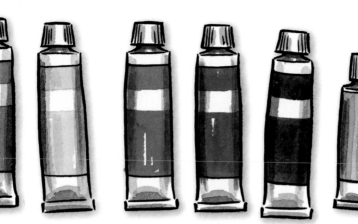

Paints

Paints are great for jazzing up a craft. Fabric paints come in a variety of colors—even in neon, metallic, and sparkles. You can also get fabric paint pens that are super simple to use! For harder surfaces, use acrylic paint, as it dries quickly and is easy to clean up. Keep a few paintbrushes on hand to apply the acrylic paint and decoupage glue.

Decorative Supplies

In addition to paints, there is an assortment of other decorative touches to choose from. Lace, ribbon, and fun trims add flair to a project. This book also introduces you to the great effects you can achieve with gems, jewels, glitter, tiles, bells, and beads. You can also personalize crafts with iron-on letters and stickers.

Baking Supplies

When whipping up critter-friendly treats and spa products, raid the kitchen for baking tools such as a mixing bowl, rolling pin, and cookie sheet. Grab measuring spoons and cups to make sure you add just the right amount of the tasty ingredients. Ask an adult for assistance when using the oven.

Please note that your pets may try to eat some of the materials suggested in the projects. Always supervise your pets when they use both store-bought and hand-crafted products to ensure their safety.

9

iPet

If you can't live without your iPod, shouldn't your pet get one too?

Materials List

- 1 sheet of 9" x 12" white felt
- Pencil
- Ruler
- Needle
- White thread
- Scissors
- Colored felt scraps
- iPet templates
- Craft glue
- Pillow stuffing
- Ribbon trim

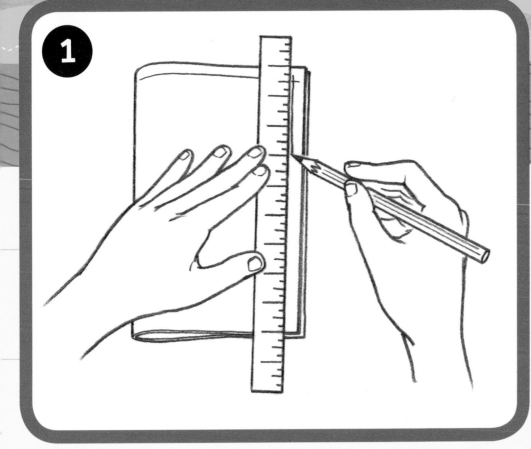

1

◄ Fold the sheet of white felt in half so that you have a 9" x 6" rectangle. With a pencil and a ruler, draw a line 1/4" in from the edge all the way around the three edges that are doubled over—you don't have to do this on the folded edge.

2

◄ With a straight stitch, sew a seam along your pencil line all the way around to within 3" of the end. Make sure you knot the thread and end your stitching. Leave this final 3" opening—this is where you will pack in the stuffing.

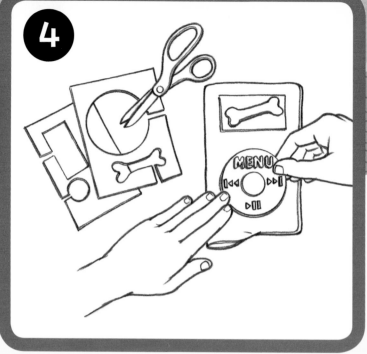

▲ Turn the entire rectangle inside out by gently pushing the felt through the opening—all of your stitching will be inside the pillow and not visible. Use the eraser on a pencil to gently push out the corners to create a rectangular shape.

▲ Cut out your smaller felt pieces in the shapes and letters that you will use for your iPet screen and controls. You can use the templates in this book (page 53) if desired. Adhere the felt decorations onto your white felt rectangle with craft glue.

◀ Fill your pillow with stuffing to make it puffy. Finish sewing your seam to secure all the stuffing inside using a straight stitch, but don't worry about the seam being visible.

6

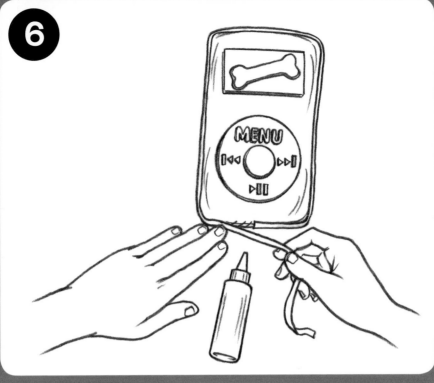

▶ Next use craft glue to secure ribbon around the entire perimeter of your iPet—you'll be covering the seams as well as the folded edge. Allow the glue to dry, and then present your pet with its new toy.

Pet Bandana

Accessorize your animal pal with the hippest pet styles.

Materials List

- Bandana
- Iron-on letters
- Ruler
- Iron
- Trim
- Craft glue
- Crown or skull templates
- Tracing paper or photocopier (optional)
- Scissors
- Pencil or white pencil/crayon
- Fabric paint
- Jewels (optional)

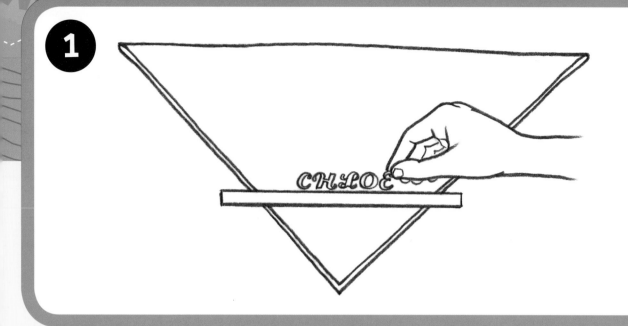

1

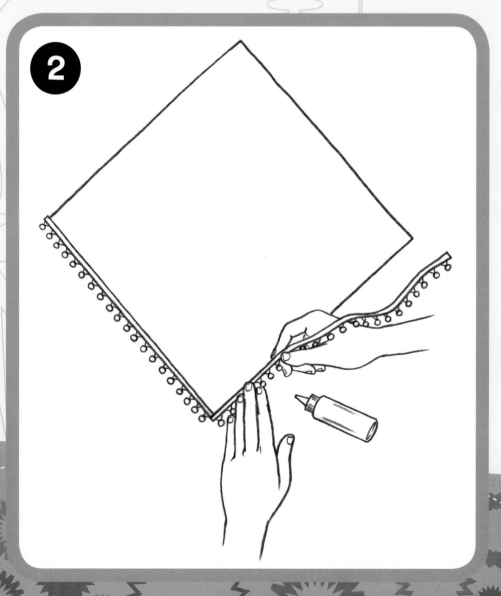

2

▲ Fold your bandana to form a triangle. You can personalize the size and look to match to your pet's size and personality. Lay out your pet's name with iron-on letters so that it fits above the tip of your bandana. Use a ruler or straight edge to space the letters evenly. Have an adult iron them onto the bandana according to the package instructions.

◄ Open up your bandana and lay it flat. Add trim to your bandana using craft glue. Let it dry completely.

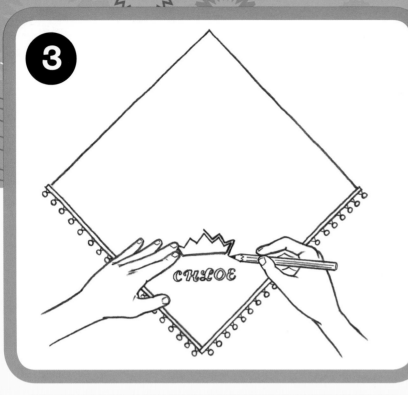

3

◀ Draw a simple outline of your desired image or use the crown or skull templates in this book (pages 55 and 57). Cut out the template or make a copy of it using tracing paper or a photocopier; you can adjust the size with a photocopier if necessary. Carefully cut out your shape and lightly trace around it onto the bandana. Use a pencil for light-colored fabric and a white pencil or crayon for darker fabrics.

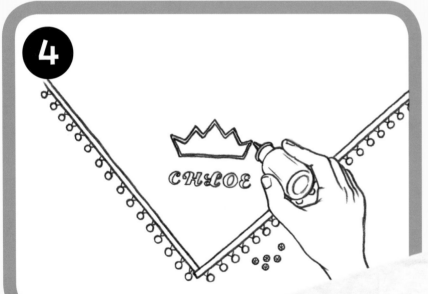

4

◀ Using fabric paint, carefully paint over the outline that you traced. (You may want to practice on paper before applying the paint to your bandana.) Let it dry completely according to the fabric paint instructions. If you wish, adorn your design with jewels.

Tiny Tee

Deck out your furry friend in the coolest critter couture!

Materials List

- Angel wing or batwing templates
- Photocopier (optional)
- Pencil or crayon
- 1/4-yard lace
- Scissors
- Cardboard
- Undershirt sized to fit your pet
- Straight pins (optional)
- Stretchy fabric glue
- Glitter or rhinestones

1

◀ Cut out or trace the angel wing template (page 59) or batwing template (page 61). You can adjust the size with a photocopier (if necessary) to fit on your pet's new shirt before cutting out the shapes. Using a pencil or crayon, trace the shapes onto the lace, and then cut the pieces from the fabric.

2

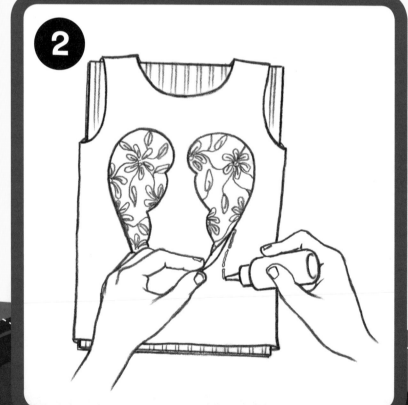

◀ Find a piece of cardboard that is about the width of the shirt and insert it into the shirt so that you have a nice flat surface to work on. You may want to pin the shirt into place using a few straight pins. Now envision an imaginary line down the middle of the back of the shirt and place the wings on either side of that line. Glue the lace wings onto the shirt, but use the stretchy fabric glue sparingly!

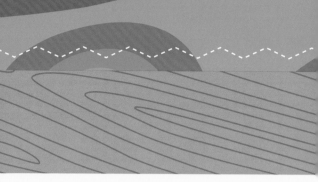

3

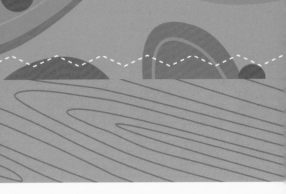

◄ If using glitter, trace each wing outline with stretchy fabric glue and sprinkle glitter on top of the glue. Be generous with the glitter; you will shake off the excess once it's dry, but you want to ensure good coverage. Allow it to dry for 2–3 days.

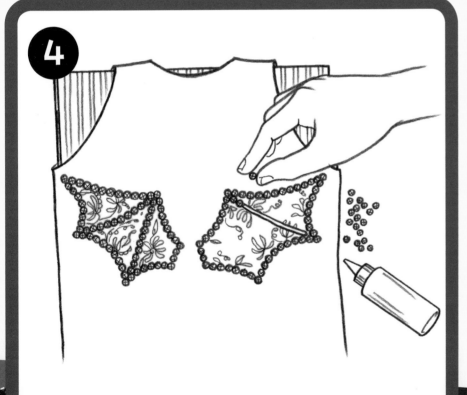

4

◄ If using rhinestones, work small sections at a time, following the wings' outline with fabric glue. Affix rhinestones to the glue lines. You may want to add some lines on top of the lace to give the wings more definition. Let it dry for 2–3 days before outfitting your pet in the latest fashion!

Paw Print Plaque

Display your pet pride with personalized paw-print plaques.

Materials List

- 1 batch dough (see recipe on page 21)
- Toothpick
- Craft glue
- Tile mosaics
- Plastic dog bone
- Acrylic paint & paintbrush
- Letter stickers
- 12" ribbon
- 20" wire

Paw-Print Plaque Dough Recipe

INGREDIENTS
2 cups flour
1/2 cup salt
1/2–1 cup water

DIRECTIONS
1. Combine the flour and salt. Add water slowly, mixing and kneading the ingredients until the mixture resembles bread dough.
2. Roll out the dough so it's about 1/3" thick.
3. Using a knife, cut out a square shape that will fit your pet's paw (about a 5" square).

◀ Make the dough and cut out your plaque shape according to the recipe directions above. Then carefully place your pet's paw in the dough, pushing down gently to ensure an even print. You'll probably want to have someone help you with this step—the more hands, the better!

2

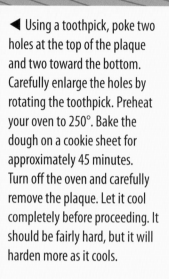

◀ Using a toothpick, poke two holes at the top of the plaque and two toward the bottom. Carefully enlarge the holes by rotating the toothpick. Preheat your oven to 250°. Bake the dough on a cookie sheet for approximately 45 minutes. Turn off the oven and carefully remove the plaque. Let it cool completely before proceeding. It should be fairly hard, but it will harden more as it cools.

3

◀ Using craft glue, attach tile mosaics around the perimeter of your plaque, being careful to avoid the holes you made. Then paint the bone with acrylic paint—you may need to use two or three coats of paint— and allow it to dry thoroughly. Once the paint is dry, attach letter stickers to spell out your pet's name.

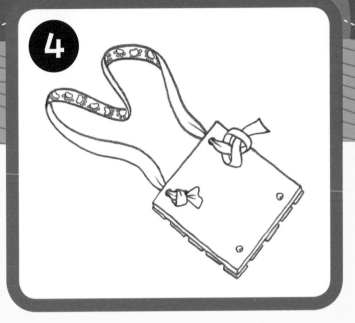

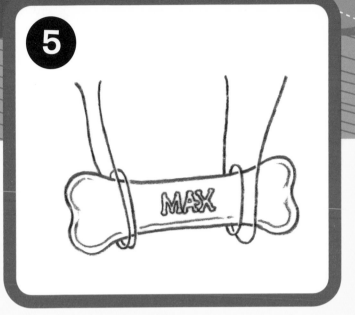

▲ Thread the ribbon through one of the top holes and anchor one end of the ribbon behind the plaque by tying several knots on top of one another. Thread the ribbon through the other hole at the top of the plaque from front to back and secure it by knotting the end. This will serve as the plaque hanger.

▲ Now cut two 10" lengths of wire. Loop a piece of wire twice around the base of the bone, and then do the same for the other end.

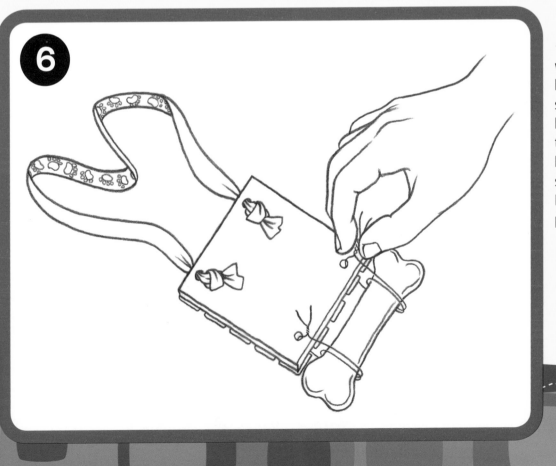

◀ Put one end of the wire through a hole at the bottom of the plaque and secure the bone in place by twisting both ends of the wire together at the back of the plaque. Do the same for the other side. Now proudly hang your plaque!

Royal Pet Carpet

Give your pet the Hollywood star treatment with this plush carpet.

Materials List

- Star template, letter shape, or other design
- Tracing paper (optional)
- Pencil
- Newspaper
- Scissors
- Fur fabric twice the size you want your carpet to be
- Marker
- Measuring tape
- Shiny vinyl, the size of your finished carpet
- Craft glue

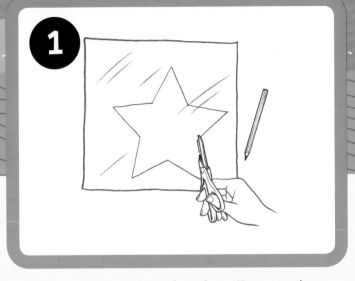

1 ▲ Determine the size and shape of your design. You can use the star template on page 63 or your pet's initials. Draw or trace the shape onto newspaper and cut it out to create a pattern.

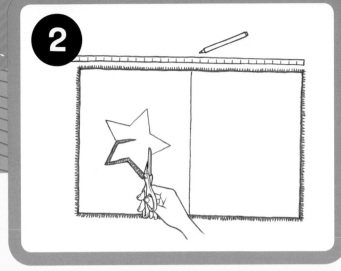

2 ▲ Lay the fur fabric on a flat surface with the furry side face down. Use a marker and a measuring tape to make a line down the middle where the fold will be. Now center the pattern on one side of the fabric, as shown. (If you are using your pet's initial(s), you will need to lay your letter template upside down!) Trace around the template with a marker, and then cut the shape out of the fur, following your marker lines.

3 ▲ Trim the vinyl to be ¹/₂" smaller around than the length and width of half the fur. Using craft glue, glue the vinyl, shiny side up, centered on top of the uncut half of the large fur rectangle.

4 ▲ Fold the side of the fur with the cut-out design down over the vinyl so that the vinyl shows through. Connect the two carpet halves securely using craft glue and be sure to press down the edges of your design.

Critter Crawlspace

Offer your curious critter hours of entertainment with this tunnel toy.

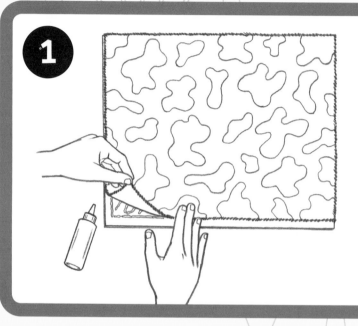

▲ Lay the poster board on a flat surface and set the printed fleece on top so that 1" of poster board is exposed at the bottom. Glue the fabric in place.

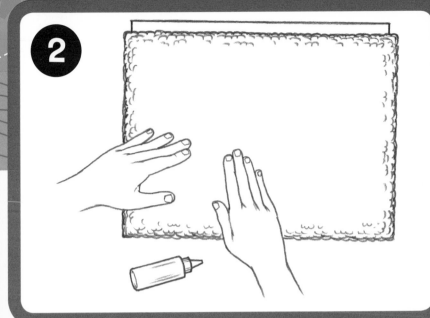

2

◀ Flip the poster board over and lay the fur fabric on top, aligning it so that 1" of poster board is exposed at the top (on the opposite side as the fleece on the flip side). There should also be ½" of fur hanging over the two ends. Glue the fur in place. Allow your project to dry before proceeding.

3

◀ Carefully roll up the poster board and line up the bare poster board strips to form a cylinder. Glue generously and secure each end with clothespins. You may need to hold the tube in place while the glue has a chance to set and dry.

4

◀ Remove the clothespins and roll back the fur to wrap the ends of the tube. Glue the fur down with tacky glue.

Window Garden

Create a fabulous garden full of fresh, homegrown delights for your favorite little friends.

Materials List

- Bucket (galvanized steel or aluminum) 6"-10" diameter
- Hammer
- Nail
- 1/4-yard fabric
- Scissors
- Outdoor decoupage
- Paintbrush
- Trim
- Craft glue
- Potting soil
- Seeds: catnip, wheatgrass, lettuce, or radishes

1

▲ Have an adult help you use the hammer and nail to poke a few drain holes into the bottom of the bucket by gently tapping the nail through in several spots.

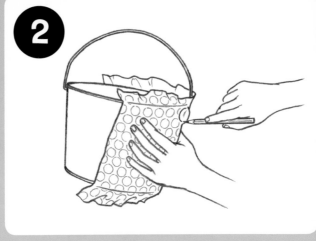

2

▲ Cover the exterior of the bucket with fabric by measuring and trimming two pieces that each cover 3/4 of the bucket's outer surface. Cut holes for the handles.

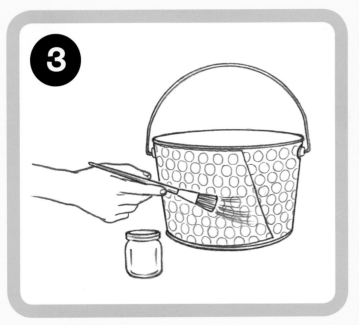

3

▲ Use a paintbrush to coat the bucket with outdoor decoupage, affix one piece of fabric to the bucket, and then cover it with another layer of decoupage. Repeat this step with the other piece of fabric overlapping the first piece. Let the bucket dry overnight. Apply two more coats of decoupage, allowing it to dry for 15 minutes between coats.

4

▲ When the fabric is completely dry, use craft glue to attach trim around the perimeter of the bucket's top edge. Again, let the bucket dry overnight. Fill the bucket with potting soil and plant the seeds of your choice! Keep the soil moist until the seeds sprout. Place the critter garden in a sunny window and water it regularly as the plant grows.

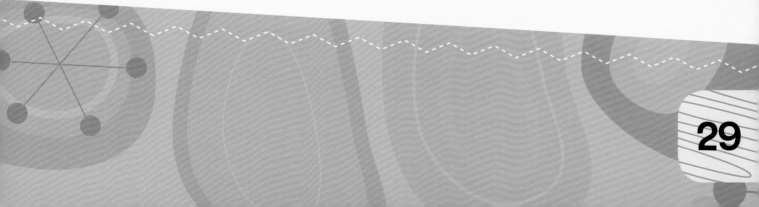

Pet Treats Tin

Create a feeding-time frenzy by designing your own charming chow cans.

Materials List

- 2 enlarged color copies of photos sized to cover your paint can
- Empty paint can
- Scissors
- Paintbrush
- Decoupage
- Colorful cardstock
- Craft glue
- Small pet toy or ornament

▲ Make large photocopies of your photos and line them up around the paint can, cutting holes to allow for the handle. Working one side at a time, use a paintbrush to cover one side of the can with decoupage, and then lay a photo on top, pressing it smooth to prevent air bubbles. Make sure that the edges are secure.

▲ Affix the second photo to the opposite side of the can, overlapping the first layer slightly to ensure a good seal. Allow the photos to dry, and then spread a thin layer of decoupage over the entire surface of the can, covering the photos completely. Allow them to dry for at least 30 minutes, and then apply a second coat of decoupage.

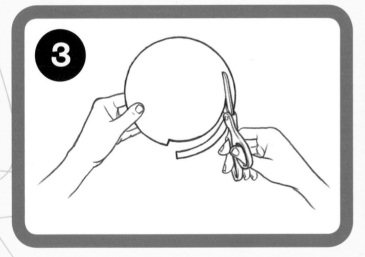

▲ Trace the can lid onto colorful cardstock, cut out the shape, and then trim it to fit into the recessed surface on top of the lid. Attach it to the lid using decoupage.

▶ Use a generous amount of craft glue to securely attach your pet toy or ornament to the center of the lid. When everything is completely dry, fill the can with your pet's favorite treats.

Petro Chic Disco Ball

Get your pet's groove on with this glitzy disco ball.

Materials List

- 18" wire
- Styrofoam ball
- Masking or duct tape
- 3 sheets black tissue paper
- Scissors
- Sparkle decoupage
- Paintbrush
- Silver wrapping paper

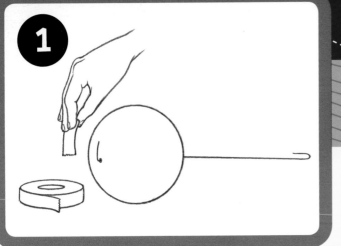

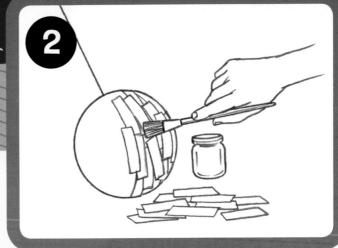

▲ Poke the wire through the Styrofoam ball, threading it through so that it comes out the opposite end and leaves approximately a 2" "tail." Secure the tail flush with the ball using masking or duct tape. You should have a length of wire sticking out of one side of the ball that will be used as a hanger.

▲ Cut the black tissue paper into several 1"x 4" strips. You'll need enough to cover the entire surface of your ball twice. Working in sections, cover the ball with sparkle decoupage. Spread and slightly overlap the black tissue paper so that the entire surface is smooth and coat it with a layer of decoupage as you work around the ball. Allow the tissue paper to dry overnight, and then repeat the process so that you have two layers of tissue. Your disco ball should look solid black and fairly smooth and even. Again allow it to dry overnight.

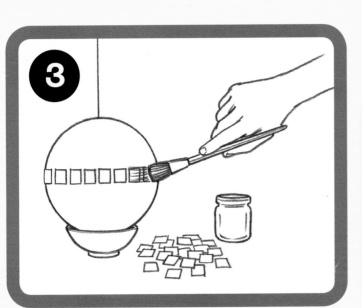

▲ Cut the silver wrapping paper into many 1" squares. Set the ball on a small bowl with the wire hanger pointing up. Use decoupage and a brush to paste the silver squares around the center of the ball, leaving small uniform-sized spaces in between.

▲ Continue to add squares, arranging them with consistent spaces, like bricks. You may need to trim your squares to fit as you work your way up and down the ball. Continue until the entire surface of the ball is covered with silver squares. Finish with a final coat of decoupage and let the disco ball dry overnight.

Bejeweled Bird Swing

Embellish your bird's cage with a sensational swing & scrumptious snack!

Materials List

- Craft glue
- 4 faceted gems ³⁄₈" diameter
- 2 wooden dowels 5" long with ¹⁄₄" diameter
- 1 yard of colorful cord
- 2 bells
- Beads
- 1 foot of ribbon
- Homemade bird cookie (see recipe on page 37)

1

◀ Use craft glue to attach gems onto the ends of two dowels. You want to make sure that the gem is slightly larger than the dowel so that is forms a "lip" to stop the cord from slipping off the dowel.

2

◀ You will be making the swing with one continuous piece of cord, so don't cut it! Starting with one end of the cord, string the bell onto the cord, loop the cord around the end of one dowel, and then tie a double knot as shown, leaving a 1" tail.

3

◀ String beads onto the long end of the cord, pulling the beads down to the dowel and tucking the 1" tail into the first few beads so that it is not visible. String the beads to a length of approximately 7".

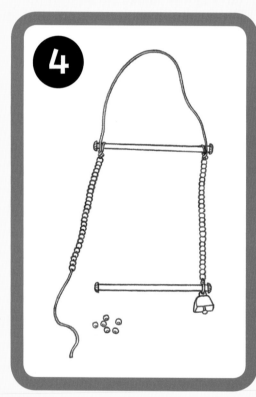

4

◀ Take the second dowel and tie a double knot at one end of the dowel. Leave 8" of cord loose, and then tie off the other end of the second dowel with a double knot. String the same number of beads as you used on the opposite side onto the remaining cord.

▶ Pull the cord tight and then wrap it around the opposite end of the first dowel once. Thread a second bell onto the cord so that the bell hangs parallel to the first bell.

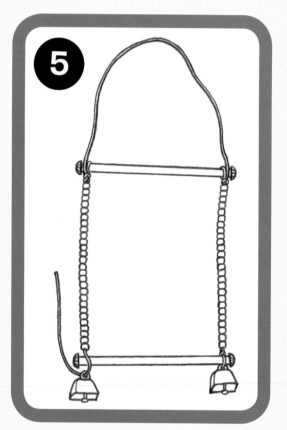

5

6

◄ Wrap the cord back around the dowel and tie it off with a double knot just under the beads. You'll need to pull the cord tightly while tying the knots. Cut the cord so that you have a 1" tail and tuck it up through the first few beads. Hang the swing in your bird's cage with a cookie. (See Bird Cookie Recipe below.)

Bird Cookie Recipe

INGREDIENTS
1 cup birdseed mix
1/2 cup crumbled Cheerios®
1/2 cup oats
1/2 cup cornmeal
1 cup natural peanut butter
1 egg
Honey
Cooking spray

DIRECTIONS
1. Mix everything except the honey in a bowl. Slowly stir in enough honey so that the mixture holds together.
2. Press the mixture into cookie cutters or mold it into shapes with your hands. Use a straw to make holes in the cookies for hanging.
3. Spread the shapes out on a cookie sheet that has been sprayed lightly with oil. Bake them for approximately 30 minutes in an oven set to 225°. When they are firm and toasted, brush the cookies with honey and bake them for three more minutes. Remove the cookies from the oven, let them cool, and hang a cookie above the swing with ribbon.

37

Precious Pet Announcement

Announce a new addition to your family or invite loved ones to a pet's birthday bash.

Materials List

- 12" x 12" printed paper (2 announcements per sheet)
- Scissors
- 8-1/2" x 11" colorful paper (4 announcements per sheet)
- Hole punch
- Patterned ribbon (10" per announcement)
- Glue stick
- 2" x 3" photos (1 photo per announcement)
- Letter stickers
- 6-1/2" x 6-1/2" envelopes

Introducing...

arlotte!

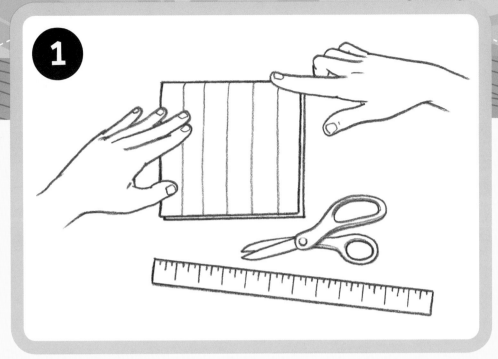

1

◄ Cut out a 6" x 12" piece of paper, and then fold it in half so you have a 6" square. You may choose to open the announcement like a book with the fold to the left, or put the fold at the top of the card.

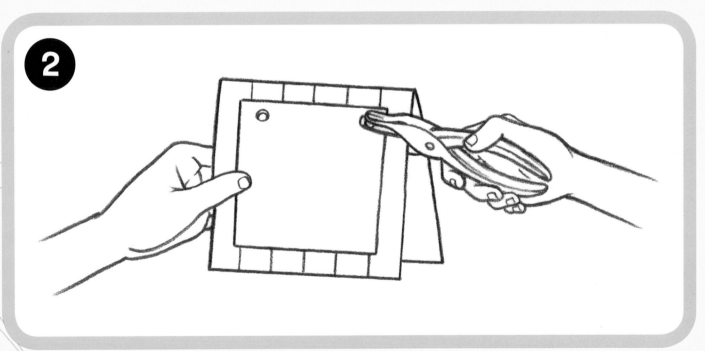

2

▲ Cut the colorful paper into a 4" x 4-1/2" rectangle. Center the piece of colorful paper on the cover of the announcement and punch holes through the top two corners of the paper and cover.

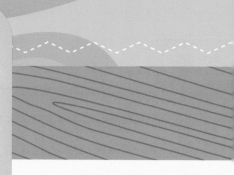

3

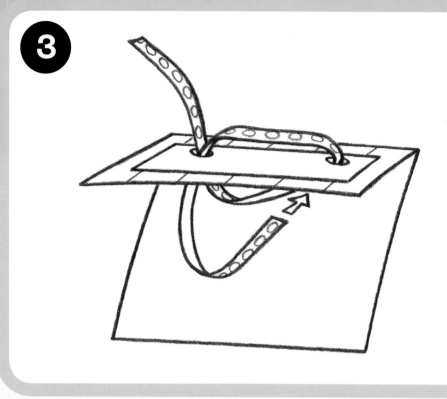

◄ Thread the ribbon down through both holes to secure the colorful paper to the cover. Pull tight from inside the card and then push the ribbons back up through the opposite holes. Leave 1" tails and cut the ends at an angle.

4

◄ Center a photo on the front of your card and glue it down with a photo-safe glue stick. Attach stickers to the card cover and interior. Fill in your new pet's information, place your announcements in envelopes, and send them to all of your friends!

Introducing...

Our Best Friend!

TIP

- Glue a photo directly on the cover.

- Use colorful brads.

- Print a message inside the announcement.

Name:

Age:

Weight:

Birthday:

Proud Family:

Posh Pet Tutu

Your graceful critter will be performing perfect pirou-pettes in no time!

Materials List

- Silver elastic cord
- Scissors
- 1 large spool of tulle
- Jewels (optional)
- Craft glue

▲ Cut the silver cord to the desired length (see sizing chart on page 52) and tie it into a circle using an overhand knot. At this point, you should try it on your pet to determine if the length is correct. You want it to fit securely but comfortably.

▲ Cut the tulle strips according to the chart. (For example, you would cut 40 strips of tulle that measure 12" long if you are making a medium tutu.) Use one cut length of tulle as your guide, and then keep cutting!

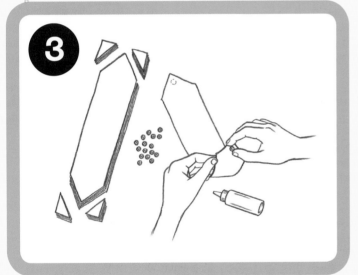

▲ Layer several tulle strips on top of one another and cut the ends into points by trimming off both corners of each end. If you want to add jewels (not recommended for smaller tutus), use small drops of craft glue to place a jewel at each point of the tulle strips, but be careful not to glue the tulle to your work surface! Turn the strips over, with the gems facing down, and allow them to dry completely.

▲ Using one tulle strip at a time, fold the strip in half and set the folded end under the silver cord. Pull the tails over the cord and down through the folded part of the tulle. Pull the knot tight and adjust the tulle tails so that they lay straight. Repeat this step for each piece of tulle, working your way around the silver cord. Be careful to always tie your knots in the same direction so that your tutu looks nice, straight, and even. Once you make it all the way around, your tutu is complete!

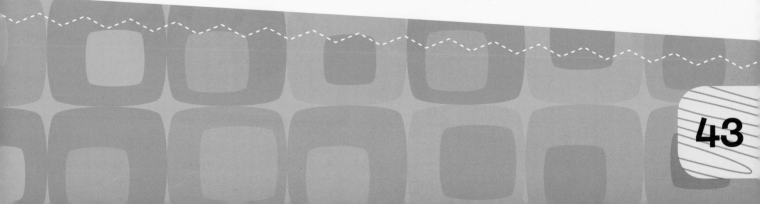

Pet Treats

Offer these healthy, homemade treats as rewards for a well-performed trick or good behavior.

Peanut Pooch Biscuit

INGREDIENTS
2 cups whole wheat flour
1/2 cup oats
1/4 cup wheat germ
1/4 cup flax seed meal
1-1/2 tablespoons baking powder
1-1/2 cups natural peanut butter
1 cup milk
1/2 cup plain low-fat yogurt

DIRECTIONS
1. Preheat the oven to 350°. Mix the flour, oats, wheat germ, flax seed meal, and baking powder in one bowl.
2. Mix the peanut butter, milk, and yogurt in a separate bowl. Slowly combine this mixture with the dry ingredients.
3. Place the dough on a floured surface and knead it until it has a consistent texture. Roll the dough to a thickness of 1/4" and use cookie cutters to cut out shapes.
4. Bake the dough on a parchment-lined cookie sheet for 15–20 minutes or until biscuits are lightly browned. Let the biscuits cool and then store them in an airtight container.

Kitty Cat Treats

INGREDIENTS

2 cups oats
1/2 cup whole wheat flour
1/4 cup cornmeal
1/3 cup canola oil
Oil drained from 6 oz can of tuna
3/4 cup chicken broth and tuna oil mixture

DIRECTIONS

1. Preheat the oven to 350°. Mix all the ingredients together in a bowl. If necessary, adjust the mixture's consistency by adding more flour or oil until the dough can be rolled out with a rolling pin.
2. Place the dough on a floured surface and knead it.
3. Roll out the dough with a rolling pin to a thickness of 1/4" and use a pizza cutter or butter knife to cut the dough into small triangles (1/4" wide).
4. Spread out the treats on a parchment-lined baking sheet and bake them for 20 minutes or until the goodies are slightly browned.

for Purrs

Little Critter Mini Sandwich Rolls

INGREDIENTS
1 large iceberg lettuce leaf
1 tablespoon natural peanut butter
4 thin peels from a carrot
4 thin peels from an apple
1 tablespoon shelled sunflower seeds
1 tablespoon sesame seeds

DIRECTIONS
1. Cut the lettuce leaf into a 4" square and spread the entire square of lettuce with a thin layer of peanut butter.
2. Spread the carrot and apple peels onto approximately 1/3 of the square.
3. Sprinkle a thin layer of sunflower and sesame seeds on another 1/3 of the square, leaving the final 1/3 of the square with just peanut butter.
4. Starting at the edge of the lettuce square with apple and carrot peels, gently roll the leaf into a long tube. Use some extra peanut butter as glue to seal the edge closed.
5. Use a knife to slice the tube into sections about 1/3" thick. (Have a grown-up help you use a sharp knife to get clean cuts.) Place the rolls in your pet's food bowl for him/her to enjoy!

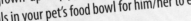

Packaging Your Pet Treats

MATERIALS
Clear plastic bags
Raffia or ribbon
Hang tags

DIRECTIONS
Place your homemade pet goodies in clear plastic bags and secure them with raffia or ribbon. Remember that an airtight package will keep your treats fresh longer! You may also wish to label your goodie bags with hang tags.

for the birds

Blissful Pet Products

Pamper your pet with these luxurious spa treatments.

Spa in a Bottle

INGREDIENTS

2–4 oz spray bottle
Distilled water
Essential oils: lavender for calming or eucalyptus for repelling fleas

DIRECTIONS

1. Fill the spray bottle with distilled water and add 2–4 drops of essential oils.
2. Spray your pet carefully, avoiding the eyes.

Bubbles Pet Shampoo Bar

INGREDIENTS
Natural olive oil and glycerin-based melt-and-pour soap base
Soap color
Essential oils
Fine soap glitter
Soap mold or cookie cutter

DIRECTIONS
1. Melt the soap base according to the package directions. When it is evenly melted, add soap color, several drops of essential oils, and lots of glitter! Stir the ingredients well until everything is mixed consistently.
2. Sprinkle a tiny amount of glitter into each mold and pour the melted soap mixture on top. Allow the mixture to cool according to the soap directions, and then pop your soap bars out of the molds!

TIP

If you are using a cookie cutter as a mold, place the cutter on a smooth surface. Push the cookie cutter down firmly as you pour the soap into the middle to prevent soap from leaking out the bottom. Let the mixture cool and then gently pop the soap out.

Sparkly Clean!
Dry Shampoo with Glitter

INGREDIENTS

Baking soda
Fine soap glitter
Shaker bottle

DIRECTIONS

1. Combine baking soda and enough glitter to make the mixture sparkle in a bowl.
2. Mix the ingredients thoroughly to spread the glitter evenly throughout, and then put the mixture in the shaker bottle.
3. Shake the dry shampoo on your pet, being extra careful to avoid the eyes. Rub the powder into the fur, and then brush the fur to remove dirt, odors, and oils, leaving behind a sparkly sheen!

Pet Lover's Agreement

I, _____, PROMISE TO PAMPER MY PET. I UNDERSTAND THAT ANIMALS NEED ATTENTION AND AFFECTION, AND I COMMIT TO CARING FOR MY BELOVED ANIMAL'S PHYSICAL, EMOTIONAL, AND FASHION NEEDS.

I, _____, SOLEMNLY VOW TO CONTINUE CRAFTING COOL ITEMS THAT WILL IMPROVE MY PET'S DAILY LIFE AND SHARING MY LOVE OF CRITTERS LARGE AND SMALL WITH THE WORLD!

_____
SIGNATURE

_____
DATE

Templates

How to use the templates in this book:

1. You may choose to work directly from the template page or make a copy of the template using tracing paper or a photocopier.

2. Cut out the shape(s) and trace around the design onto your project.

TIP

You can make the design larger or smaller by adjusting the size settings on a photocopier. Ask an adult for help if necessary.

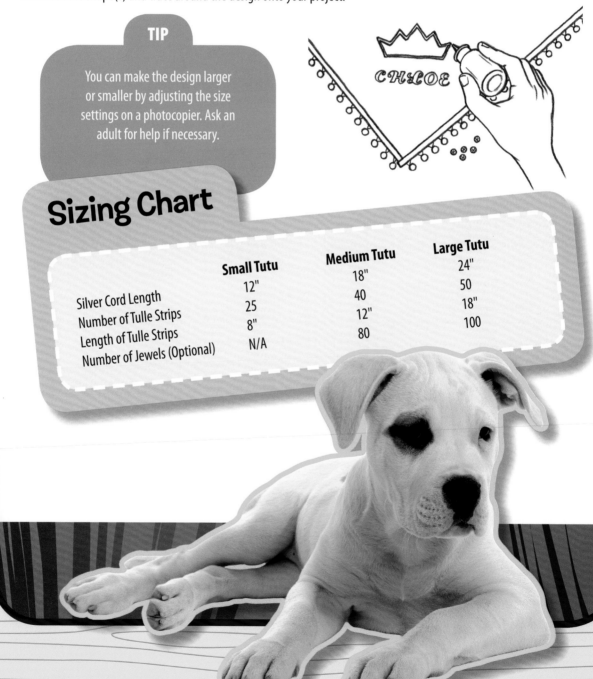

Sizing Chart

	Small Tutu	Medium Tutu	Large Tutu
Silver Cord Length	12"	18"	24"
Number of Tulle Strips	25	40	50
Length of Tulle Strips	8"	12"	18"
Number of Jewels (Optional)	N/A	80	100

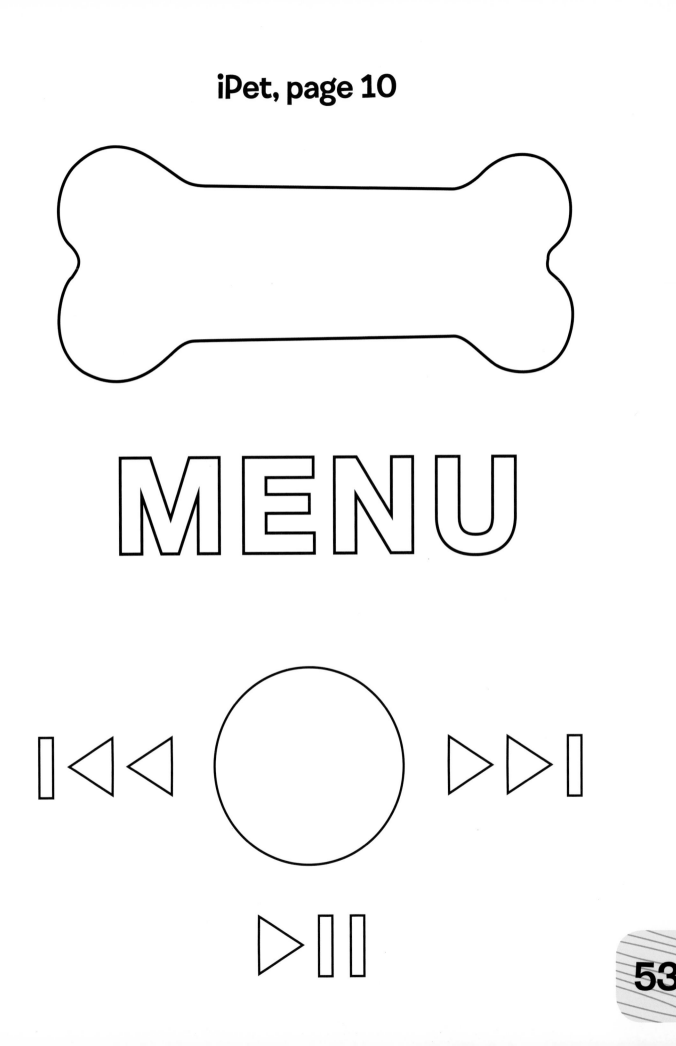

MENU

Pet Bandana, page 14

58

Tiny Tee, page 17

60

Tiny Tee, page 17

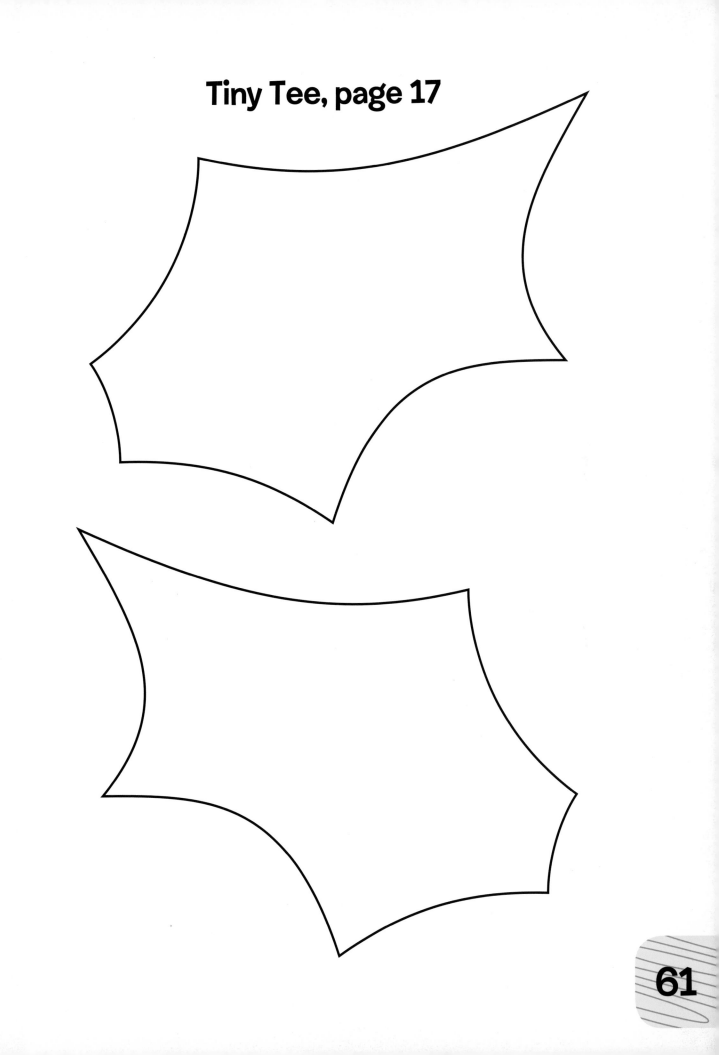

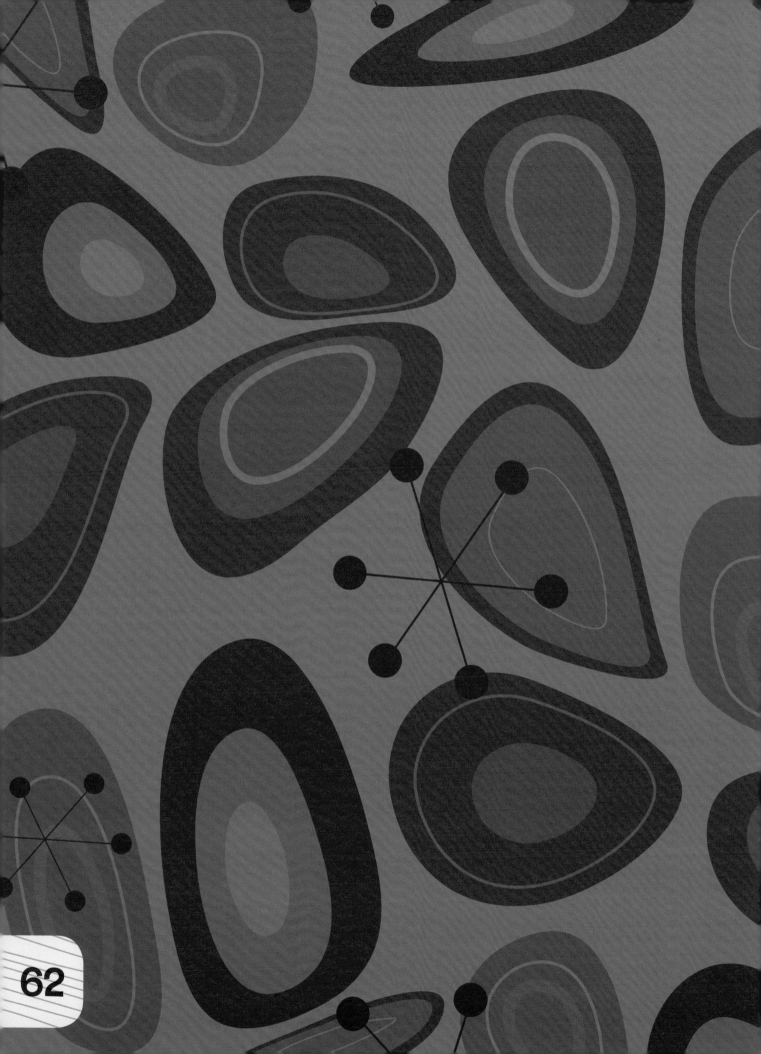

Royal Pet Carpet, page 24

64